written by
Mi
with Paul Brenner M.D.

cover design by
Joyce Brenner and Susie Reneau

calligraphy by
Susie Reneau

Mi*

* *pronounced me*

Library of Congress
Catalog Card Number: 83-81837

First paperback edition, 1983

ISBN: 0-914135-00-7

other books
by
Paul Brenner M.D.

Health Is A Question Of Balance
Life Is A Shared Creation

Rainbow Medical Clinic
P.O. Box 2986
La Jolla, Ca. 92038

And in the pure light of the silence and the sound the Pure Breath rested.

In the beginning of the eighth movement of The Symphony of Life, there is Stillness, Sound, Harmony, Melody, Rhythm, instruments of harmony, instruments of melody, and then a Pure Breath followed by a burst of pink-orange light.

A whole note is born.

The Pure Breath breathes the
whole note's song.

The whole note and the song
are called "Mi". *

The Pure Breath dreams a special
dream within Mi.

Mi accepts everything the Pure
Breath dreams.

The dream is not simple. The
dream is not easy.

Mi sings the dream in the Pure
Breath's garden and plays with
flowers, rocks, and trees.

* *pronounced me*

And at times Mi is the flowers,
the rocks, the trees.

Mi flies.

Mi sings in melody.

But all too soon Mi finds it is
no longer alone.

There are other notes.

Mi listens to its own note, and then
the sound of the other notes.

Mi tries to sound like the other
notes, but its sound is not
the same.

Mi feels less than the others.

Mi becomes very, very sad and wants to be more.

Mi makes its first sound of disharmony.

One day the note makes a wish, a wish to be like the other notes, a wish to be more than just Mi.

The Pure Breath breathes within Mi, "You are perfect just the way you are."

Then the note hears another voice, a voice different from the Pure Breath.

This voice is from outside the note.

"My name is 'I'. I will tell you
how to be more than just
a note.

In this lifetime, you have the
gift of six choices.

You have chosen one --
that is, to be 'Mi.'

Five choices remain.

Your dream to be more depends
on what I have to say.

Listen very carefully!

When you use the mystical, magical name 'I', two doors will appear: The Door to Somewhere, that offers more, and The Doorway to Anywhere, that holds no promise.

When these doors appear, you must make the choice to walk through one of the doors or to stay as you are."

The voice from outside becomes silent.

Mi is confused.

Mi has no memory of having made a choice, and wonders what to do.

Mi sings out to the Pure Breath
for an answer.

The Pure Breath breathes within Mi,
"If we knew all the answers
we would not need you. You
are free to do whatever you wish.
But always, always remember, Mi,
you are worthy."

The note is confused by the inner
and outer voices and by what
they have to say.

In silence, Mi, the note, wonders,
"Who is I, and Who is We?"
and then says aloud, "I wish
to be more!" -- OOPS!

In the moment of using that
mystical, magical name "I",
two doors appear: The Door
to Somewhere, that offers more,
and The Doorway to Anywhere,
that holds no promise.

Very slowly, the note goes through
The Door to Somewhere.

The voice from outside the note
says, "Remember, you have
many choices. Become more.
Take bars from the sheet music
and string your whole note".

The note strings itself with bars
upon bars of music.

The note becomes "more".

In a burst of golden yellow light,
the note sees itself in a mirror.

Mi is cradled by thirty-four golden
strings made of golden threads.

"The note" is now a harp, the most
beautiful musical instrument
of all.

Now as the Pure Breath breathes
within Mi, Mi plays all the
music of the other notes, and
more.

Mi calls itself, "Mi, The Harp".

Mi creates all its strings; this harp
can do all things.

Mi, The Harp, will show those
other notes what it can do.

So The Harp plays its own special
music to all the notes that
will listen.

As The Harp grows older, it travels
further and further from home,
and in time finds there are
other harps with other strings
that can do just as many things.

Mi, The Harp, no longer feels special.

Mi says, "I want to be more!"
-- OOPS!

In the moment of using that mystical, magical name "I", two doors appear: The Door to Somewhere, which offers more, and The Doorway to Anywhere, which holds no promise.

The Harp does not hesitate this time and walks through The Door to Somewhere.

The voice from outside The Harp says, "Take more bars of music and add strings to your harp. Then take sheets of music and wrap yourself tightly, very, very tightly.

The Harp wraps itself and wraps
itself and wraps itself with
sheets of music.

The Harp becomes "more".

In a burst of forest green light,
The Harp sees itself in a
mirror. The Harp is cradled
by eighty-eight golden strings
made of golden thread, and
enclosed by a most beautiful
forest green, wooden wall.

The Harp is now a piano, the
grandest musical instrument
of all.

Now as the Pure Breath breathes
within Mi, it plays every
possible note, every sharp,
every flat, every scale.

Now, Mi is more than a simple
harp -- Mi calls itself, "Mi,
The Grand Piano".

Mi creates its own wooden wall;
this piano is the grandest of all.

Mi, The Grand Piano, will show
those other harps what it can do.

So The Grand Piano plays its own
special music for all the
harps that will listen.

In time, Mi becomes so big, so heavy,
so grand, so safe in its wooden
wall, that Mi can no longer
move, see, hear, or feel anything
at all.

Mi, The Grand Piano, can only see,
hear, and feel itself.

Mi wonders, "What good is it to be
so grand?"

Oh, how Mi longs for "the good
old days."

To be grand can be very, very lonely.

Mi wonders, "What good is it just
to give music and never receive
music?"

Mi listens for an answer to its
question.

Not a sound from the Pure Breath
or "You Know Who" is heard
through the thick, dark wall
that encloses Mi.

Again, Mi wonders, "Maybe walls
are for those who cannot receive."

In time, Mi does not feel very grand, or even very beautiful, but ugly, dark, lost, hapless.

Mi knows what "woe is me" means.

In that dark moment, Mi remembers the words of the Pure Breath: "You are perfect just the way you are. If we knew all the answers, we would not need you. You are free to do whatever you wish. But always, always remember, Mi, you are worthy."

Mi still does not understand.

Mi cries out for the Pure Breath to breathe an answer.

Mi ponders, who is the Pure Breath, who is "We" and who is "You Know Who?"

No one answers and no one can be heard through the thick, dark wall of the piano.

That night Mi goes to sleep wishing for answers, wishing for understanding.

Mi dreams that it is a note, alone, on a sheet of music.

In the dream there are flashing lights.

This is a special dream that seems familiar.

Tears of joy stream down Mi's face as Mi smiles a smile and giggles a giggle.

Then a voice from within the
dream says, "Be serious! Be
serious! All that ever was or
will be depends on your journey."

Mi slowly rises off the sheet music
and begins to fly through space
beyond the stars and through
all the perfectly tuned notes
heard since the beginning of time.

Mi feels part of all those notes
and is bathed in love, a love
that has neither a beginning
nor end, a love beyond love.

Mi feels unworthy of such love and
wonders, "Why me...why me?"

Still within the dream, Mi hears
another voice, the voice of the
Pure Breath: "Your journey is
not only for you... you are but
one note in Life's Song...
try to live your dream."

The journey continues.

Mi comes before all the notes since
the beginning of time that are
out of tune and is frightened
when these notes block the path.

Mi slowly smiles when it recalls
all the times it too was off key.

In the moment of acceptance, all
the out-of-tune notes giggle
in perfect harmony.

These notes part and Mi continues
on the path.

Suddenly, Mi finds itself before a
huge door.

The Pure Breath breathes, "You are
before The Door to Everywhere,
and are about to enter The
Chamber of the Most Exalted Notes."

Mi finds itself alone in a room
of pure light whose walls are
made of that light.

The room is lined with rows upon
rows of soft, puffy, charcoal gray
bars of music, nothing else,
not even a single musical rest.

The room is silent beyond silence
and still beyond stillness.

Mi wonders, "Where are the most
exalted notes -- where is their
music?"

Mi hears a voice from behind... a voice with power, a voice that Mi never heard before, a voice that is part of Mi:

WE WILL ALL REST AT ONE
FLY "IN" LIFE TO THE SUN
WHEN EACH NOTE ACCEPTS
IN TRUST
THE "WE" THAT IS "ONE"
IN "US".

When the voice finishes, Mi, with respectful knowing, slowly backs out of the room, shaking uncontrollably.

Mi floats backward through space and stars, and during the journey sees one of the notes that it hoped to find in The Chamber of the Most Exalted Notes.

"What are you doing among the stars?"
Mi asks.

At that moment, Mi is drawn into
the other note.

They fuse.

They are one.

They part.

The journey continues and the
dream ends.

Mi's eyes open, only to find it is
still a grand piano, but now a
piano that knows joy.

"That is a dream beyond dreams and
more real than real."

Within moments, Mi is breathless and
feels a crushing, choking heaviness.

Mi cannot move or breathe.

Mi fears it is going to die.

Mi cries: "Why have a dream like
that and die?"

Mi calls for help, but there is no
one to help poor Mi.

In that death-filled moment, Mi
knows the only one who can
save me is me.

And in that knowing, Mi breathes
easier.

Mi then says the sentence aloud, "The only one who can save me is me."

Mi breathes still easier.

Finally, Mi repeats the sentence even louder.

"THE ONLY ONE WHO CAN SAVE ME IS ME -- BUT WHO AM I?" -- OOPS!

In the moment of using that mystical, magical name "I", two doors appear: The Door to Somewhere, that offers more, and The Doorway to Anywhere, that holds no promise.

Mi does not want to be more, but at the same time, no longer wants to remain a grand piano.

Mi strains and strains and strains and painfully drags itself through The Doorway to Anywhere.

There is no voice from the outside, no voice from the inside, no instructions -- nothing.

Mi finds itself in a dark, black tunnel.

Mi is frightened, very frightened.

Mi holds on to Mi and gazes into
the darkness, and sees a soft
blue light at the end of the
tunnel.

Mi moves slowly toward the light
and, with each step, becomes
lighter and lighter.

As Mi approaches the blue light, it
hears the most beautiful harp
music of ALL.

Mi enters a room of soft blue
harps, then turns to see itself.

Mi is no longer a piano, but now a
harp; not a golden harp, but
a soft blue harp.

Mi remains silent.

Mi does not want the other harps
to know that the most beautiful grand piano of all once felt ugly, dark, lost, and the most hapless of all.

In silence, Mi receives music from outside itself and finds the sound to be beautiful.

In that silence, Mi, The Harp, can hear.

Silence is also a time to see, a time to feel, a time to smell, and a time to taste the music of Life.

Beyond Mi's control, Mi's harpstrings move, and play the same music to which it listens.

Mi no longer wants to be more than the other harps.

But, when Mi, The Harp, thinks
about being the piano that
felt ugly, dark, lost, hapless,
Mi becomes still.

In moments of Mi not loving
Mi, Mi loses its harmony
with all Love.

Mi cannot turn away from the
ugliness without turning
away from the beauty.

Mi cannot turn away from the dark-
ness without turning away
from the light.

Mi cannot turn away from the past
without turning away from
the present.

The harp is all of its strings, those
tuned and those untuned.

How can Mi accept the other harps
if it cannot accept itself?

With this Knowing, Mi welcomes the
Pure Breath within and in a
clear voice, sings aloud the song
of its journey.

Mi sings of its dream, of its walk
through the black tunnel of
darkness into the light, of its
shame, of its beauty.

Mi sings its song to all the harps.

When the song is finished, Mi
experiences love.

Through receiving, giving and understanding, Mi begins to relearn life's harmony.

Mi begins to accept all things, including Mi.

Mi, The Harp, dances and sings with the other harps.

Mi holds onto their love and they need Mi.

So Mi rests within the soft blue light of love.

However, in time, Mi again has difficulty breathing.

Mi, The Harp, is haunted by the words of the Pure Breath: "But always, always remember, Mi, you are worthy."

Mi wonders out loud, "If I make another choice, can there possibly be even more love?"
-- OOPS!

In the moment of using that mystical, magical name "I", two doors appear: The Door to Somewhere, that offers more, and The Doorway to Anywhere, that holds no promise.

Mi, The Harp, stops in the middle of its dance, sits in the middle of the soft blue harps, and cries.

The harps beg Mi not to choose either of the doors: "Please, please stay as you are."

And then the harps sing:

Please stay here with us,
Oh, Mi, please us.
Please stay here with us,
Oh, Mi, be just like us.

Almost beyond Mi's control, as if in a dream, Mi slowly walks through The Doorway to Anywhere, muttering, "You are worthy, you are worthy. Remember, Mi, you are worthy."

This time, there is no voice from the outside, no voice from the inside, no instructions - - - nothing.

Once again, Mi finds itself in a dark, black tunnel, but this time Mi is not frightened.

Mi is in search of more love.

Mi sees a deep purple light at the end of the tunnel and runs toward the light.

With each step Mi becomes lighter and lighter.

At the end of the tunnel, Mi hears the most beautiful symphony of ALL...

"The Symphony of Life".

Mi is breath-filled with silent
joy and love.

But as Mi turns, it sees itself.

Mi is no longer a harp, but now a
note, not a whole note, but a
deep purple half note.

Mi is ashamed at being a half note
and feels less than Mi.

Mi is hollow.

In breathless silence, the joy and
the love are drained into
hollow stillness.

Then Mi remembers:

it cannot turn away from its
ugliness, without turning
away from its beauty,

it cannot turn away from its
darkness, without turning
away from its light,

it cannot turn away from its
past, without turning away
from its present.

Mi cannot turn away from any
part of Mi without turning
its joy and its love into hollow
stillness.

In understanding, Mi welcomes the
Pure Breath within and breathes
the half note's song.

This song and its rhythm come from
Mi's own understanding of Mi's
special journey.

As a half note, Mi can be many things--
a note within a note, a note with-
in a harp, a note within a grand
piano, a note within the instru-
ment of love itself.

Mi is a part of The Symphony of Life.

The different songs of the different
notes from the different journeys
are the music of The Symphony
of Life.

Mi is an understanding old half note and sings its special song to all the notes that will listen, and all the notes that will not listen.

But Mi, in all of its joy, in all of its wisdom, does not know all things.

In time, fewer and fewer questions are asked and fewer and fewer answers are given.

Once again, Mi sings and plays in love's garden and rejoices with the flowers, rocks, and trees, and, at times, Mi cannot tell the difference between itself, the flowers, the rocks, the trees.

But Mi still cannot fly.

Mi gives itself sadness when it leaves the present moment and returns to other times as a whole note, as a harp, or as a grand piano.

The sadness leaves when Mi returns to the moment.

However, Mi is driven by a searching, often lonely need for other half notes.

In that need, Mi finds many other deep purple half notes.

The notes are drawn to each other
by some mystical, magical "something", and when these notes
come near to each other they
form a bridge, and tune one another.

During and after each tuning, the
notes make a sound that is
more than either half note can
make by itself.

In those love-filled moments, Mi
is both Mi and more than Mi.

Mi bridges and is bridged by thousands upon thousands of deep
purple half notes.

During such mystical, magical moments of love, the notes find their special place in The Symphony of Life and sing their special song:

Now in love, in love be here.
Now in love, in love be.
Now in love, in love.

In these high-pitched moments of love, Mi, as if made of delicate crystal glass, quakes and shatters with the release of its own special love.

In such moments, Mi dissolves "in" love.

"In" love is a love without end, a love that has neither a beginning nor end, a love beyond love.

Once before Mi experienced a similar love, but cannot remember where or when.

Mi plays in the harmony and the
melody of deep purple love.

But in time, the searching and the
loneliness return to drive Mi
to sing in pure disharmony
once again.

Mi questions, "What was my first
choice? What will be my last?"

Mi is ready for anything and asks:

"Who is We? and Who am I?"

This time, there is no "OOPS"

Mi is aware of its question and
is ready for its sixth and
final choice.

In the moment of using the mystical, magical name "I" for the final time, two doors appear: The Door to Somewhere, that offers more, and The Doorway to Anywhere, that holds no promise.

Both of these doors are partially open and edged in pure light.

But this time there is another room.

This room has no door.

Mi unhesitatingly enters the room without a door.

The room holds only five bars
of music.

Mi is on the top bar and does
not Know what to do.

Mi chooses to step down an octave.

Mi turns around, and from the
bottom bar of music hangs
a golden sign -- Doorway
to Nowhere.

In a flashing moment of light,
Mi steps up a new octave on
an entirely new sheet of music.

Mi has no idea of where it is, or
even how it got there.

Suddenly, a familiar love bathes Mi.

Mi recalls its dream as a grand
piano and now remembers
where it experienced "in"
love before.

Mi, in flashing light, tears of
love streaming down its face,
smiles a familiar smile, and
giggles a familiar giggle.

Mi slowly rises off the sheet
music and begins to fly.

Mi feels very, very special:

"My journey's over -- to be 'in'
love is so simple, so easy".

Mi, still feeling unworthy of such Love, wonders, "Why me?... why me?... but who am I?"

The Pure Breath sighs within Mi, "We are one... we are all exalted notes. I is Mi and Mi is We. Remember, your journey is not only for you. You are but one note in Life's Song. Try to live your dream."

Mi questions, "But how can 'I' be 'we'?"

The Pure Breath breathes, "It is not necessary for you to replace your own 'I' with another's 'I.' Let die that part of the 'I' that is not you, and let die that part of the 'we' that others say you should be. Just be your self. Remember, you are perfect just the way you are. If we knew all the answers, we would not need you. You are free to do whatever you wish. Remember, Mi, you are worthy. You were created in OUR SOUND, in the sound of ALL LIFE, in the harmony of oneness, and in the melody of aloneness." (1-33)

Mi stammers, "But... but am I
really worthy?"

The Pure Breath laughs and laughs
and laughs. "Oh, Mi, how soon
you forget."

Mi also laughs and then cries in
the light of understanding:
I AM I AND I AM WE...
I AM... I AM THAT I AM!
I AM THE SOUND!"

Mi hears its sound, and
Mi hears that it is good.

Mi now knows that since the very beginning it creates its own stillness, its own sound, its own music: its own harmony, its own melody, its own disharmony, its own rhythm, its own instruments of harmony, its own instruments of melody, but is still just one note in Life's Song.

In a burst of ultraviolet light, Mi returns to The Symphony of Life as an ultraviolet note.

The Pure Breath breathes within Mi, "Welcome home... wake up to life."

Mi is no longer just a note within the instrument of love but now a note within Life.

Love is but one great instrument within Life and within Mi.

Mi plays in Life's Song and plays in the ultraviolet garden of Life.

Mi Knows who "Mi" is.

Mi accepts, but not always with understanding, the notes that wish to be more and do more.

Mi Knows, but often forgets, that the desire to be more, be more, to do more, do more, is the driving sound behind melody's rhythm.

Yet this desire to be more, be more, to do more, do more, is the heartbeat that drives The Symphony of Life to continue its open-ended creation of harmony.

In loving silence, Mi feels the struggle of the searching and often lonely notes, and patiently awaits the sound of their journey.

However, Mi does not always sing blissfully ever after, or in perfect harmony.

Mi gives itself sadness in moments when Mi hungers for affection or feels unworthy of Love.

Mi gives itself sadness in moments when Mi is in the hollow stillness of self rejecting abandonment or questions it's acceptance by another.

Mi gives itself sadness in moments when Mi tries too hard to be more than Mi or feels less than Mi.

Mi gives itself sadness in moments when Mi drives Mi to do more, do more, or feels "Mi" does not do enough.

Mi gives itself sadness in moments when Mi beats Mi to be more, be more, or feels "Mi" has no drive, no rhythm, no thing.

Mi gives itself sadness in moments when Mi is in the limitless, boundless, soaring freedom of prolonged aloneness, or in the limited, bounded, suffocated, bridged, flat moments of prolonged togetherness.

Mi gives itself sadness in moments when Mi longs for the past or dreams of the future.

Mi gives itself sadness in moments when Mi ponders creative choice or questions if there is any choice at all.

Mi gives itself sadness in moments when Mi Knows all the sounds, all the harmony, all the melody, all the musical parts of all the instruments of the Pure Breath, or is not sure of even its own note, its own sound, its own tone.

Mi gives itself sadness and confusion in those moments of self-doubt when Mi judges Mi, yet knows exactly how others should be.

Mi gives itself prolonged, locked moments of sadness and misunderstood disharmony when the special sound of a once bridged note is never heard again, and in a silent moment, LIFE reclaims life unto ITSELF and so becomes nourished.

Mi cannot turn away from moments of death, without turning away from the next moment of birth.

Mi cannot turn away from any part of Life without turning away from all of Life.

However, Mi learns with difficulty that disharmony is no more than misunderstood harmony.

These moments of disharmony drive Mi, as does Love, to reclaim Mi's own birthright, to live and to be nourished by the true Mi, the note that is One within Life.[26, 27, 29-31]

When Mi is in the moment, when Mi accepts in trust "you", "we", "they," "flowers", "rocks", "trees", "us", then the "I" within Mi becomes many and Mi becomes "One in Us".

And in loving all things, Mi creates many great instruments within itself of harmony.[21]

The loving of all things teaches Mi oneness.

Yet there are other moments when Mi needs to hear its own separate part, its own melody within The Symphony of Life.

Mi also finds Mi within Mi.

Mi hears its own special melody by listening to all the individual tones, all the voices within Mi that compose its perfect note – (9-13) the pure note that Mi was born to be. (26,27)

Mi tries to blend all those pure notes, all those pure voices, into sound and silence.

But when Mi tries to be any other sound than the sound Mi was born to be, and tries to be what others say Mi should be, Mi loses its melody by singing off key.

Mi must be true to Mi.

When Mi is in the moment, when Mi accepts in trust all the parts that make up Mi: all the individual tones, all the voices, then the "We" within Mi becomes One.

And in self love, Mi creates its own unique instrument of melody.(24-25)

Self love teaches Mi to rise above the fear of separateness, the fear of aloneness, and rest into all oneness. (20,24)

However, it is not that easy or that simple, but difficult and hard for Mi to understand, or even accept, all Mi's imperfect voices, all Mi's imperfect tones as part of Mi's perfect note within Life's Perfect Song.

In those rare moments when Mi accepts its imperfectly perfect wholeness, then Mi can stop its judging and its trying and Mi can rest at One.

And in such rare moments, Mi unwraps itself from its blanket of hollow stillness and flies on the wings of Love.

Mi rises above its own melody.

Mi's greatest peace, Mi's greatest joy, Mi's greatest rest, be it at times of oneness, be it at times of aloneness, is in the Now-Here -- the rarest moment of all.

When Mi is in the moment THERE IS LIFE and the many within Mi become One.[3a]

Mi, as if made of delicate crystal glass, quakes and shatters with the release of its own special life, a life without end, a life that has neither a beginning nor end, a life beyond Life.

When Mi is in The Moment, Mi dissolves within the Pure Breath.

In such mystical moments, Mi lives its dream, a dream of love, a dream of understanding, a dream that is sung in the sound of the Pure Breath, a dream that is sung to all the exalted notes who question their self worth or fear to be within Life.

In such magical moments, Mi, just one note in Life's Song, soars into open-ended, always evolving Life.

And Mi sings:

WE WILL ALL REST AT ONE
FLY "IN" LIFE TO THE SUN
WHEN EACH NOTE ACCEPTS
IN TRUST
THE "WE" THAT IS "ONE"
IN "US".

And Mi heard everything that it had sung, and behold, it <u>was</u> very good.

And the silence and the sound <u>continue</u> Life's unfinished song.

Author's Note

The most difficult work in The Symphony of Life is not only to find your true note, but to live your true note.

But your journey and mine, move us and every single note that was ever heard, or will ever be heard, much closer to The Door to Everywhere, The Chamber of the Most Exalted Notes, and the music of ALL Life.

I wish to thank you for just being you.

To ALL Life,

Mi

P.S. Can you possibly imagine what the next movement in The Symphony of Life will be?

Reference Notes

1. In the beginning, the Pure Breath created harmony and melody.

2. And melody was without sound and absent; and silence was blanketed by hollow stillness. And the life force of the Pure Breath played with the unheard sounds.

3. And the Pure Breath breathed, Let there be sound: and in a burst of infrared light, there was sound.

4. And the Pure Breath heard the sound; that it was good: and the Pure Breath separated the sound from the stillness.

5. And the Pure Breath called the sound Music and the stillness Silence: and in a burst of red color, the stillness and the sound completed the first movement in The Symphony of Life.

6. And the Pure Breath breathed, Let the yet unheard sounds be creative and let the desire for more sound separate the sounds.

7. And the Pure Breath separated the yet unheard sounds that were more creative from the unheard sounds that were less creative: and it was so.

8. And the Pure Breath called the more creative unheard sound Harmony. And in a burst of orange color, the silence and the sound completed the second movement in The Symphony of Life.

9. And the Pure Breath breathed, Let the remaining unheard sounds be grouped together and let these sounds be heard: and it was so.

10. And the Pure Breath called the less creative unheard sounds Melody, and the melody within melody the Pure Breath called the Tones of melody: and the Pure Breath heard that it was good.

11. And the Pure Breath breathed, Let melody mature and yield tones from within itself and voices in Key not unlike the Pure Breath, whose tone is within melody: and it was so.

12. And melody matured and yielded tones from within itself and voices in Key, not unlike the Pure Breath, whose tone was within melody; and the Pure Breath heard the melody: that it was good.

13. And in a burst of yellow color the silence and the sound completed the third movement in The Symphony of Life.

14. And the Pure Breath breathed, Let there be sounds within harmony, sounds to separate the music from the silence; and let these sounds be heard forever and ever.

15. And let the sound of harmony be heard within melody: and it was so.

16. And the Pure Breath created two great sounds of harmony, one to be heard in music and the other, a lesser sound, to be heard in silence; the Pure Breath made the sounds of silence also.

17. And the Pure Breath placed the sounds of harmony into music and into silence, and so into melody.

18. And the sounds of harmony separated the sounds of music from the hollow stillness; and the Pure Breath heard the sounds of harmony and the sound of rhythm: that it <u>was</u> good.

19. And in a burst of green color, the silence and the sound completed the fourth movement in The Symphony of Life.

20. And the Pure Breath breathed, Let there be instruments to play in life, instruments <u>that</u> may rise above melody into the open-ended creation of harmony.

21. And the Pure Breath created great musical instruments and every kind of playing instrument for Life. Their sound brought forth even more sound. And every instrument of harmony was like the Pure Breath: and the Pure Breath heard that it <u>was</u> good.

22. And the Pure Breath blessed the instruments, breathing, Mature, and increase in number and fill the melodies with all kinds of tones and let the musical instruments of harmony spread throughout melody.

23. And in a burst of blue color the silence and the sound completed the fifth movement of The Symphony of Life.

24. And the Pure Breath breathed, Let there be instruments to play melody in life, large instruments and small instruments like the Pure Breath: and it was so.

25. And the Pure Breath made musical instruments of melody like itself, large instruments and small instruments that played the sound of melody: and the Pure Breath heard that it <u>was</u> good.

26. And the Pure Breath breathed, Let us make notes in our sound, in the music of the Pure Breath. And let these notes be heard over the tones within melody and over the instruments of harmony and over the instruments of melody.

27. So the Pure Breath created notes in its <u>own</u> sound, in the sound of <u>ALL LIFE</u>, in the music of Life notes were created: in the harmony of oneness and in the melody of aloneness.

28. And the Pure Breath blessed the notes and the Pure Breath breathed into the notes, Mature, and add to and nurture melody and quiet it; and be heard over the tones within melody and over the instruments of harmony and over every living thing that plays in melody.

29. And the Pure Breath breathed, Behold, I, the We that is One, has given you every tone that is heard in melody and every voice that is needed for your growth and maturity: to you melody will be nourishing.

30. And to every instrument of melody and to every instrument of harmony and to every thing that plays within melody, THERE IS LIFE. I have given to you all the beginning tones for your nourishment: and it was so.

31. And the Pure Breath heard every sound that the Pure Breath had made, and behold, the sound was very good. And in a burst of ultraviolet light the silence and the sound completed the sixth movement in The Symphony of Life.